G000129957

KATHLEEN RAINE

ON A DESERTED SHORE

FRONTISPIECE BY GAVIN MAXWELL

THE DOLMEN PRESS
LONDON : HAMISH HAMILTON

Set in Pilgrim type, and printed and published in the Republic
of Ireland at the Dolmen Press, 8 Herbert Place, Dublin 2

1973

Published in association with Hamish Hamilton Limited
90 Great Russell Street, London WC 1

THE DOLMEN PRESS
SBN 85105 248 7

HAMISH HAMILTON
SBN 241 02404 8

© 1973 Kathleen Raine

Anima est ubi amat, non ubi animat.

The faint stars said,
'Our distances of night,
These wastes of space,
Sight can in an instant cross,

But who has passed
On soul's dark flight
Journeys beyond
The flash of our light.'

I said, 'Whence he is travelling
Let no heart's grief of mine
Draw back a thought
To these dim skies,

Nor human tears
Drench those wings that pass,
Freed from earth's weight
And the wheel of stars.'

7 September 1969

ON A DESERTED SHORE

WHERE my treasure is
A grave :
My heart also
Empty.
                    Sorrow
Is its own place, a glass
Of memories and dreams; a pool
Of tears. Narcissus pale
Sees his own drowning face.

2 · From the hollow sphere of space
Echo
Of a lonely voice
That cries, my love, my love :
I do not know
Whether I spoke or heard
The word
That fills all silence.

3 I hid my heart
Within a certain stone
In a far mountain burn,
World-egg in its blue shell,
Invulnerable until
That pebble crushed,
Power and life were gone :
Not where we live but where we love, the soul.

4   What substance had Euridice,
    Or shade?
    Unseen he knew that she was near
    Whom when with bodily arms he held
    Was waterfall, was fleeting flame, was empty air :
    Yet in that country far
    He only cast a shadow, bright was she.

5   I cannot weep
    Who, when I turn to you in thought
    Behold a mystery so deep,
    A world upheld upon a breath
    That comes in life and goes in death
    Troubling dark leaves upon a starry bough.
    Who dreams our lives I do not know,
    Nor in what land it is we meet.

6   Memory : beyond recall
    The linnet's song,
    The clover-scented air;
    Yet we were there,
    My love and I together in one house.
    Home is the sum of all
    The days that sheltered us;
    The place of no return.

7   Should some angel, turning the leaves
     Of the closed book of lives
     Open again those days solitary and sweet and wild,
     Would not some essence pass, some chord
     Tremble into the harmony of the spheres,
     Lingering overtone of the remembered music that was
          ours?

8   The great whispering-gallery
     Sends back strange echoes.
     The desolate sends out a cry,
     And there comes an answering voice
     That utters the heart's mystery :
     Does any heart reply?
     Do we hear
     The sea in the sound of a shell held to the inward ear?

9   How deep the recollection of the dead
     In whose great memory we recall
     The fabled story;
     We taste the bitter fruit, we fail, we fall,
     While earth's myriad buried hearts
     Murmur forever in our ears
     Music of undying joy.

10   *Night. Moon. Black leaves.*
I open the French window wide :
Between us other barriers,
Invisible, infinite.
On my threshold
When my window is open upon the night,
Moths, black leaves, moonlight.

11   *Many and one : in the great memory*
We know as we are known,
And you and I
Near as being to itself. Why then do we,
Waking to an ignorant day
Hear only in sleep
Sweet island voices that make us weep?

12   *We who from day to day depart*
From the country of the heart
In death return
To the fields our feet have travelled, our tears sown :
Sleeper beneath the rowan-tree,
You have become your dream,
Sky, shore, and silver sea.

13   We do not hear the harmony
That sounds about us everywhere;
Sense bleeds on iron and thorns
Of rock and fire
Until death breaks the elemental forms
To free the music of the spheres
That builds all worlds continually.

14   They pass into that music :
I too in sleep have heard
The harmony sublime
And known myself among the blessed dead.
We cannot walk the waves they tread,
For the earth of heaven is sound,
To sense this stony ground :
They hear as music what we feel as pain.

15   Under the budding boughs
Beyond a grave he stood :
She took him for the gardener who mows
The springing grass,
But then saw, he it was
Who grows the living from the dead.

16 I like a traveller have passed
    Through days and years
    Stranger and guest of many lives,
    And came at last
    To my love's place and time,
    Dreamed I had come home,
    But waking stood by a grave-side.

17 A grave :
    Loves' bitter fruit
    And buried seed,
    Sanctuary inviolate
    Of unborn life.

18 No title mine to mourn —
    From my own memories exiled
    Since you on later friends bestowed
    Those regions of your dreams and mine
    Interwoven in one world.
    That finespun texture rent,
    Invisible sanctuary torn down,
    Where but in sorrow shall I hide?

19   *If many, how lonely,*
      Even in requited love how far
      Each heart from other;
      But if one the whole, and we
      Leaves on that great tree,
      And weary time a flow in starry veins,
      Nourished from hidden roots, and blossoming boughs
      Where birds of heaven rest,
      Then no love lost.

20   *Rigid, naked, pale —*
      Body's friend and guest,
      Where now your abiding-place,
      Gentle wandering soul?

21   *Cold comfort for the heart :*
      I read the books, I acquiesce,
      Plotinus on the soul's descent,
      Iamblichus on the Mysteries,
      The Indian, German, and the Greek :
      Knowledge a cold mirror where forms pass
      That only seem to move and speak.

22 Mist-dwellers :
    Love in part remembers,
    But who we are,
    And where before our eyes had met —
    In soul's far wanderings
    What is that glory we forget?

23 In heart's truth I declare
    What most I fear
    To find beyond death's veil :
    Not legendary hells of ice and fire
    But a face too merciful
    For my own devil-peopled soul to bear.

24 So far —
    Out of the night
    We travelled, you and I,
    To meet on this small star.
    Our chosen fate,
    Our meed and sole desire
    All we have lost.

25   Not to be unbarred :
     I beat upon the gate,
     And every way the dark :
     Bands I cannot break,
     Hooded hawk
     Of my spirit.

26   People of dreams :
     As in a glass we meet,
     Darkly : I the ghost whose haunt
     Is your bright fields.

27   When empty seas and winds and distances
     Divided us
     I still could turn my face
     And say, that way he lies.
     I have no compass now
     To tell me where beyond the multitude of stars
     Lost Paradise.

28   *Enough the day — had I, a child*
      Under the wide sky
      Happy when petals opened or bird sang
      Foreknown my human part,
      That I must hurt and harm
      And bring to naught,
      Never had I known joy.

29   *Unseen fingers cool as hyacinth-roots*
      Dislimn the clay
      Or soul's long-loved discarded mortal face :
      She of graves,
      Whose secret alchemy
      Brings all our ends to her immaculate source.

30   *How many faces have you worn,*
      Life after life,
      By human passion
      Obscured and torn? None
      So dear, my love,
      As I knew by your name.

31   Water of life
     That wells from some deep vein
     Beneath the graves,
     Beneath the roots of sorrow —
     Music its flow :
     Whence comes whither goes
     Joy, whose source none knows?

32   Not mine the joy
     That pours its melody
     Over my rocky bed : how long its flow
     Before the stone I am turned to
     Is worn away?

33   Mountain and tree and bird,
     And that pure stream —
     How beautifully the world
     Mirrored back to us
     An ancient dream :
     The dreamer gone,
     Nature an empty glass.

34 Away, away,
    Unhealing time,
    Since you can bring no day
    When my love and I,
    Though I should wait life-long
    On lonely shores,
    Can meet again.

35 Banished from that bright dream
    Of the heart's truth,
    Betrayed by all that we have done and been,
    Sorrow still keeps faith.

36 Truth comes full circle
    As departing light
    From infinite space
    Returns to the heart
    Still what it was,
    Embracing all.

37   *Truth is echo's voice*
In whose resonance
Question answers question,
Hate to hate replies,
Confusion to confusion,
Cry to cry cries.

38   *Despair — we approach but never reach*
That quiet place.
The suicidal leap
Invokes a mercy earth denies :
It is hope
That wakes to anguish
And will not let us sleep.

39   *Hope and despair — the scope*
Of what we are,
Height and deep
Each mirroring other :
Infinite desire
The far fall we fear,
Heaven, hell, the angel's ladder,
The dead man's drop.

40   Blessed who mourn,
      For love is comforted
      In every station of the heart :
      It is enough
      That on the stone of earth
      The print of feet.

41   How many buried hearts
      Instruct me when I speak
      Of that long pilgrimage
      The soul must walk
      On bleeding feet
      Who has in folly lost
      One whom in bitter after-wisdom she must seek.

42   So many scattered leaves
      The Sibyl shakes
      From the living tree.
      Gather who will her oracles,
      Believe who may —
      All truths are lies
      Save love to love in love replies.

43   Lost Paradise
     With all its trees adrift
     In the great flood of night,
     And I live yet
     Not knowing where in emptiness
     Landfall lies.

44   A night in a bad inn —
     But I would say
     Guest in love's house;
     And blessed and thrice blest
     Who walk on earth's sweet grass,
     Bathe in time's stream,
     And under green boughs rest —
     Too short a stay.

45   For the beat of a heart
     A world, a dream endures,
     Yet on this earth we met,
     And every stone is dear
     That wounds love's pilgrim feet
     Walking the way of time's
     Six thousand years.

46 Longing of lips and thighs —
    A grave apart,
    For arms' embrace too wide,
    Or fingers' touch.
    The language of the flesh
    Too faintly cries :
    And yet no lover lies
    As the dead so close at heart.

47 Strange bird across my evening sky —
    Who, passing soul, your guide
    On that far flight
    Beyond earth's dwindling star?
    With certainty of strong desire
    You wing your traceless way
    Into harbourless night.

48 They shall be comforted, he said,
    Who sent the comforter
    To those who mourned him, dead :
    What comfort could he send,
    He being crucified,
    Unless himself, who died?

49 *The last sorrow silent —*
  Forgetfulness
  That feels no loss,
  No hope discerns,
  Saddest impoverishment
  When deepest memories fade
  And all love's tears are dust.

50 *Dear angel of my birth,*
  All my life's loss,
  Gold of fallen flowers,
  Shells after ebbing wave
  Gathered on lonely shores
  With secret toil of love,
  Deathless in memory save
  The treasures of my grave.

51 *Time was*
  When each to other was a glass,
  And I in you and you in me beheld
  Lost Paradise,
  With every tree and bird so clear
  Regained it seemed :
  We did not guess how far
  From the heart's mirror the reflected star.

52   *Illusion all —*
Yet where for us the real
Unless what seems?
These cloud-capped towers
More durable than brass
Our dreams.

53   *Say I must recognize*
I but imagined love
Where no love was,
Say all is a dream
In whose brief span
Childhood, womanhood, the grave
Where my love lies :
That dream is all I am.

54   *Cast not before swine —*
The rational animal
Oysters' soft aphrodisiac flesh prefers :
Who values then a pearl
At so great price
As to sell all
To purchase one?

55   Mussel-pearls
     From Sandaig shore
     Held in a shell
     As God worlds
     In the palm of his hand :
     These our treasure,
     Sea-life's toil,
     Seed more rare
     Than barren sand.

56   What infinitely precious thing
     Did we seek along the shore?
     What signature,
     Promise in pearly shell, wisdom in stone?
     What dead king's golden crown, tide-worn,
     What lost imperishable star?

57   Silence of the dead;
     The untold :
     What would you have me say?
     Dear love, when we on earth kept house together
     Were you then this mystery?

58   If fancy cannot cheat
     The fevered flesh, the aching heart,
     Can sense the dream
     With lineaments of dust?
     From Paradise
     The bird's undying voice
     Sings on.

59   She who in cold elemental arms upbore
     Her prince to shore
     Yet did not win his heart
     Bought dear these mortal feet;
     Must pay love's price : how else
     Shall an immortal walk in sorrow's ways?

60   I would not change my grief
     For any joy :
     Sorrow the secret bond
     The signature of blood
     That seals to you my life
     Indissolubly.

61   From long ago returned,
     As my lost self you seemed :
     Of lover's play what need
     For children gazing in a stream
     Bright head by golden head?

62   Ah, burning boy,
     In winter's night
     To me you came,
     You seemed to supplicate, but I,
     Reaching with mortal arms to your cold fire,
     Could not come near
     Your place of pain.

63   I see you in mind's eye,
     A man of light;
     How faint and far away
     Your face that blesses me.

64   *Image of an image, shade of shade,*
      In memory or dream,
      Time future or time past,
      In this or any world or state of being,
      Shall we who parted
      Meet at last?

65   *Sea-change :*
      The grain of pain
      Love layer on layer enspheres;
      Sorrow its gradual pearl
      Perfects with life-long toil
      Beneath the tides.

66   *Dark stream.*
      I did not know
      When to your brink I came
      How full your flow
      Of the world's sorrow :
      I dip my cup and drink.

67   *A prison, a paradise —*
Tell me, dear friend,
Beyond those gates never to be unbarred, where pass
A people of dreams,
This world, which now it seems?

68   *By dreams uncomforted*
I wake to this blank day :
Free-will, fixed fate.
Foreknowing providence,
And life astray,
All possibility
Narrowed to this weary bed.

69   *Already it has changed —*
Dear love, you would not know the place.
I look for you in memory's house,
But there too rooms grow vague.

70   Yellow iris by the shore,
       Burnish of wing and golden eye,
       Green-gold birch and, gold on water,
       Sun's bright rings hand could not hold,
       You will not see this spring, nor I,
       Nor in the bay the rocking eider.
       All wasted and all spent, that gold.

71   Heart's memories —
       Rooms I cannot enter more,
       Green ways by the water :
       Joy once ours
       Sings in the wind that stirs the grass.

72   Always just beyond —
       The next wave will lift its deep-sea treasure to the strand,
       The next flower open golden centre, stone be star.
       And yet the near how far
       From whose green sanctuary
       The ousel flings its wild wind-drifted song.
       From body's blindfold free,
       Have you, lost seeker, found?

73 We were of a kind, nearer
    You were than brother,
    Whose hand clasped mine,
    Now dust; your land
    Beyond the heart's dark night.

74 Of a kind, living and dead;
    For as you are, or are not, all must be;
    And if the dead be not,
    How came you here, my child,
    With wisdom in your heart, and crowned with joy?

75 Little of what you were, less of myself I knew,
    Loved with my blind heart I knew not who,
    Nor from what root love's recognition grew,
    Who in my ignorance worshipped and wounded you.

76   *What the hand holds —*
So little of time's flow
The all we know;
But from their hearts who pass,
The lifelong moment breaks
Into death's boundless now :
Shelterless their state, and ours.

77   *Arid bilbergia's rigid leaves*
Describe each its parabola. Slow the flow
Water takes from air, air from swirling space,
Comes to its term, to standstill dies.
As above, so below,
Traced by figures of the dancing stars.

78   *Shadow of hills on the still loch, mysterious*
Inviolate green land, whose sun is cool as water,
Whose stones bruise not,
Seems soul's native place, this weary road
The dark country in a glass.

79   *Your garment cast away,*
       This body's clay
       The grave that shrouds from sight
       The man of light,
       Bright, but how far you are.

80   *Flash again, golden wing,*
       Across my sterile plot,
       Seeking in vain
       Similitude of glade and dell.
       Where human passions dwell
       Few flowers spring,
       Too far from that remembered hill.

81   *If I could wake*
       From bitter life as from a dream,
       In innocence new-born
       To see the first day break,
       The promise of the eternal dawn
       Would bear your name.

82 Original sin :
   I stand condemned, being born,
   To cast the human shadow;
   We darken each our sun,
   Who have not done, but are, that wrong.

83 Two wanderers in a single dream
   By paths of gold on silver seas
   We to lost Paradise came home,
   Together stood beneath those blossoming trees,
   But went our ways
   Uncomforted, and each alone.

84 Memories : shrivelled leaves
   To keep or throw away.
   Love cannot piece by piece
   Remake the felled tree.

85   From your grave-side
     All ways lead away,
     And time is long, my love,
     And memories fade,
     Old hearts grow cold :
     Must I too break faith
     With joy?

86   Sad and strange
     Are the dreams of the old,
     Joyless and cold
     Those chambers underground.
     Ghost among ghosts I range
     Catacombs of the mind
     And neither find nor seek,
     Nor laugh nor weep.

87   Hard is the way
     To your unvisited house,
     Barred the gates. Some say
     To love is given the key
     Of memory, the grave, Paradise.

88   *This empty world too small,*
     Heart's void too great,
     Everywhere visible the wall,
     Nowhere the gate.

89   *'Till death us part,' the young promise :*
     Too short a wedding-day.
     Life parted us; too long a loneliness
     For those who wait
     Outside love's sanctuary.

90   *What mist falls between*
     Two who have seen
     One in other the eternal face?
     What violation
     Shatters the bright mirror
     Lover holds to lover,
     Or blindness darks the glass?

91 Does that Judgment seem less dread,
    The Judge more merciful,
    Each being to ourselves
    Accuser and accused,
    And heaven and hell?

92 All seems the same;
    But this familiar room
    Stands in the years we shared,
    Where I, a ghost
    Out of this unreal future, haunt
    The long-past present that was home.

93 Heart's truth : from shelving depths
    Shaped by the weight of sorrow where it broods,
    Sightless surfaces,
    Tormented by the sun,
    Love's monster weeping form.

94   Heart's truth : a moment out of time,
      Pollen-grain adrift,
      How small and fine,
      Golden upon the spirit's breath
      Into that quiet chamber sown.

95   The resurrection of the dead :
      Into what strange land
      Are you, beside whose empty grave I stand
      New-born, my child?

96   Heart turns into its night
      Scanning the darkest quarter for the dawn
      Of a sun that set :
      Else there is none.

97 *If I could turn*
   Upon my finger the bright ring of time,
   The now of then
   I would bring back again.

98 *Since smoke rose from your pyre*
   All clouds are dear; but how
   Among those vague bright forms,
   Yours shall I know?

99 *'In spirit accompany me.'*
   — Your parting words by heart I know.
   On what far journey then do we
   Into the dark together go?

100   Into your boundless state
          All night afloat
          On lift and fall of the great sea
          Rocks in the bay my anchored boat.

101   As myself; so once
          When hand in hand.
          I here, you in no place
          That such as I can find,
          Living and dead,
          Still of a kind.

102   Beyond the empty door
          Spaces, distances, stars
          Innumerable, beautiful and far;
          Mysterious night over us.
          The darkness too His house, and ours.

103   Out of the arms of night
       None can fall,
       Refuge of sinners
       Whose merciful stars towards us
       Beam from their height
       Indifference
       Absolving all.

104   Ended my earthly day,
       And with averted face
       I from your graveside turn away
       Into a veiled, a secret place.

105   Over your mountain isle
       Streaming cloud
       Shrouds the sunset :
       A shawl drawn close
       Over a mourner's head.

106   Great the domain of love :
      Farther than eye can see
      From my small house of life
      Realms of your new state encompass me.

107   Sun gives no light
      And days like shadows pass.
      Shut by the lids of sense, my blinded gaze
      Cannot discern your spirit bright.

108   Cadence of an old song from Eriskay
      Tells the heart's story :
      From dissonance of the world I turn away
      Not to evade but to descry
      Lineaments of humanity.

109 Grief's metamorphoses :
Anguish, small pregnant seed,
Becomes a worm that gnaws through years,
At last quiescent lies; not dead;
Till waking, what winged impulse takes the skies?

110 'Made to be broken,' a lover said
Who knew the heart
That breaks and breaks again,
And yet will not believe
That love is born to grief.

111 Not sorrow breaks the heart
But an imagined joy
So dear it cannot be
But we have elsewhere known
The lost estate we mourn.

112   *Whole that has made me,*
      Whose stress and weight
      Creates and will destroy,
      Each part, I find,
      Bears always all the world.

113   *Downcast on the ground,*
      The form of spirit
      We are but do not know
      Save by a shadow
      Distorted, earthbound.

114   *You who cast no shadow, nowhere, everywhere,*
      All that you loved you are,
      Sun's gold on the sea, waves far out from the shore,
      Flowing for ever.

115   *Blue serene wide sky*
Where sight runs free, joy
Of unbounded light :
It is as if we meet.

116   *Dream, shadow of hope and fear,*
Secret foreshadower, guide
Of all souls, living and dead,
What the unwinding and inwinding thread
But heart's desire?

117   *I am content to be*
At last what first we were,
Grass of the one hill,
Water of the one pool,
Breath of the same air,
Sight of the single eye.

118   The Nine Nicks rose out of the past
Into this after day.
'You have been long away,'
They said, 'can you forget
We in his life had part,
Speak to you from his heart?'

119   We walked in the same dream :
Do you, awake,
Dissolving clouds recall of hills once home
That sheltered us in sleep
Whose desolate ways I tread alone?

120   At the last leap I shrink
From fall of black sea-cliff and moiling water, wake
To find in gray of dawn vague leaves and roses break
In foam of that far sea.
On lip of petal, margin of leaf, that brink.

121   *Somewhere, it seems,*
You who walk with me in sleep;
But in the sand of dreams
Your passing leaves no trace
To follow or find that place.

122   *If I could follow you,*
How find?
In number's starry flow
Of all night's multitude, what lot
Once cast us heart to heart?

123   *Ah near at heart :*
Far star's reflection in a well
Is still
Light.

124   *At the end of fear*
Out over that black skerry,
Regions of wind and moiling sea :
How long will mortal terror
Withhold, imprison me?

125   *If hope could dare*
All heart's desire
Bright hills how fair
Despair would build
In empty air.

126   *Whisperer in the wind —*
From what dream do you look upon this shore
Grown strange and fair and far?
Rain walks with heavier tread,
In rustle of grass you are,
Then not — .

127   Near and far, summit and sky,
      Soaring wing, circling joy,
      Thrilling bird-voice over the bay,
      You their bright presence,
      Dazzle of blue waves' dance,
      Gold of the silver sea.

128   Opening a vanished door
      I move on insubstantial feet
      About your window, desk and chair,
      Reviving each familiar object there.
      Do memories of the living build
      Memory-houses of the dead,
      A place at heart where we may meet?

129   That we die who live
      My heart knew by your grave.
      Does he live who died?
      'He is not here,' the angel on the stone replied.

130   *Faith, shadow of desire*
Some hold; but I
Who angelic hearsay fear
To live by,
Yet know that only the listening ear
The gazing eye
Can the far descry.

Suddenly the trees looked strangely beautiful :
'It has taken the form of trees,' I said,
'And I of a woman standing by a burn.'
So near I stood to your new state
I saw for a moment as you might
These sheltering boughs of spirit in its flight.
Shall you and I, in all the journeyings of soul,
Remember the rowan tree, the waterfall?